# MARKS OF A CHANGING CITY

JAKE HAMPSON

ISBN 978-1-956010-78-7 (paperback)
ISBN 978-1-956010-79-4 (hardcover)
ISBN 978-1-956010-81-7 (digital)

Copyright © 2021 by Jake Hampson

All rights reserved. No part of this publication may be reproduced, distributed, or transmitted in any form or by any means, including photocopying, recording, or other electronic or mechanical methods without the prior written permission of the publisher. For permission requests, solicit the publisher via the address below.

Artist's name: Katherine Sutton
Photographer: Kristie McLean

Rushmore Press LLC
1 800 460 9188
www.rushmorepress.com

Printed in the United States of America

# CONTENTS

Chapter 1:   City Changing into New.......................1
Chapter 2:   Drastic Change..............................11
Chapter 3:   Walk to School..............................15
Chapter 4:   Old Experience Changed To New...............20
Chapter 5:   Art With Old but New Teacher................23
Chapter 6:   Break to Prevent Overload...................30
Chapter 7:   Martial Arts for Gym........................34
Chapter 8:   Counseling With Old Ally....................37
Chapter 9:   English With New Spin.......................43
Chapter 10: Home to Brother.............................47
Chapter 11: Walk Away to Real Home......................53
Chapter 12: Art With Friends............................56
Chapter 13: Heading to Sell Art.........................61
Chapter 14: Setting Up at the Fair......................64
Chapter 15: Selling Art to Old and New Teacher..........68
Chapter 16: Surprise at The Fair........................72
Chapter 17: Sales to Old and New........................77
Chapter 18: What is Happening...........................84

Glossary................................................87

All italics in the book between characters communicating is in sign language. This will mostly be done, as shown below. Italics will also be used to show emphasis mostly in one word uses.

*Hello, my name is Mark. How are you doing?* Signed Mark.

# CHAPTER 1

## *City Changing into New*

My name is Mark. My parents hate what my city is changing into. The change started when I was young, just entering preschool. I have few memories of that time, but I could still see the slow new reality forming over the course of the years. I guess, to many, it was going too fast. Still, the full effect and goal didn't reach completion until many years later. Only looking, back after all these years, was I able to see the change.

My parents would tell of the changes happening and how bad they were for our community. The mall changed to have more sensory-friendly music, more level floors and, to my parents' horror, a sensory calm-down room. My parents didn't think anything needed to change, as they thought people were able to go to the mall before without any problems. They hated the changes because they made conditions more sensory-friendly but not more physically accommodating. The mall did add more ramps, but it had many large inclines where the stores were situated on the outside. Inside there were tight turns around different sales kiosks and corners. My parents didn't understand the concept of sensory problems. They didn't think they existed, figuring they were just in people's imagination. When my friends' parents would take me with their kids to the mall, they would praise such changes. Back then, I didn't know the reason for the changes happening to the city, but now I do, and I am grateful for them.

Parks changed; many of the older play structures were removed, in favor of ones with ramps to move around the play structures instead of stairs. Some had both stairs and tunnels to different areas, with small puzzles on ground level. Indented sandboxes were set into the ground with a curb and a ramp to help people with disabilities to get into the sand. My parents actually loved these changes, as they helped more people to be able to play and make friends. Libraries changed, adding many more audio and braille books to their shelves. Story hour now had people who spoke sign language, so more visitors could know what was being said. They had people reading books in different languages at different times.

As time passed, many students obtained individualized education programs (IEPs) or 504s. These plans were designed to help students to succeed, even if they had differing skill levels. IEPs were for people who needed special education help; these students would be evaluated to check on the Students who had 504s or IEPs. A 504 was just required accommodations for people who didn't need special education. Teachers who did not accommodate students with such plans would be forced to leave. Most made visible accommodations, such as for people in wheelchairs or those missing body parts; not so much for the less-visible ones though.

My family approved of those teachers and would be startled and angry when they learned one of the teachers was forced to leave. My family was against these changes, as they thought someone shouldn't need help if they were physically able and should be able to function on their own. They thought that about people whose disabilities weren't obvious to the eye. I didn't understand that perspective and still don't know why they have such an opinion, but it is what they believe.

In the past, I thought it was normal that people shouldn't get help if they didn't have a visible disability, but my teachers told me otherwise. Who was I to believe back then but my parents? It took me changing to the perspective of my new city and getting diagnosed to realize that they were wrong. This started when they first started talking to me like others who had a mental disability or delay and refusing to help with the problems they didn't view as existing.

People were moving into the city because it had changed to become more accommodating. More people were moving in who had what society called a disability. I was raised knowing the term by a different word, one I shouldn't and won't repeat. Every school's staff in the district encouraged all the kids to play together and try to include everyone in various activities as much as they physically could. Many parents would also join in if they were volunteering on that day. One popular activity was hide-and-seek; the adults would seek most of the time and let the kids hide to the best of their ability. Another game involved chasing a teacher around the playground; one would work with the slower kids and another one with the faster kids.

The first time I remember realizing what was happening was when some of my early friends I met through my parents were leaving.

I didn't know why they left until later, but by then I had mostly forgotten them. My friends were moving because their parents didn't want to be in a city that accepted what they viewed as make-believe disabilities or one's people were lying about. Many disliked how the city was growing to be more diverse overall and hated how people could work with what those parents viewed as "less effort."

My parents wanted us to move, but we couldn't because of the jobs they had, jobs they wanted to keep. My parents made chairs for people with back problems, special tableware for people with weak jaws or sensitive teeth, and different wheelchairs for various levels of mobility. My parents wanted to help others with what they viewed as "real problems" and not ones that were made up.

The adults of the town consistently received new training from those who were trained in working with people with special needs, for physical, mental, or emotional reasons. There were many different people giving each training, and they all helped each other. Some training was in how to help with panic attacks, sensory overload, or seizures. Many more trainings were given on allergies and how to include people of varying skill levels and abilities. My parents always complained, asking why they needed to learn to accommodate such things as panic attacks or sensory overload. This was how I was raised, to be ableist in certain situations. I don't know where my parents learned this idea, but I think it might be out of hatred for how they see others getting easier jobs while they needed to work harder.

I saw changes in teachers; after different training sessions, their behavior around other students changed, either for better or worse. I saw the changes happening but didn't realize what they meant. The place I lived was changing quickly, shifting to a new world perspective. The city I was in was the first to adopt these changes, but all over the country, many more were adopting such differences and becoming more accommodating.

Changes started in the schools and quickly spread throughout the city. This was all because of one group of people campaigning to make a dream happen—a place for people to thrive. This led to part of the city hearing their plea and acting to help. In this case, it was to the benefit of those who needed accommodations to succeed. The group was formed mostly of teachers and parents. Mr. David, my old art teacher, helped to lead the group, along with the other teachers.

The group mostly disbanded after reaching their goal and getting the laws and motions passed. Many of the people are still advocating in different schools for more help for students like me and a few others whose parents don't support accommodations. Many went to the state and national levels to try to get more help by campaigning during their free time. This jumpstarted many of our neighboring cities to also change and adapt over time to help more people.

My parents would continually complain as this was happening, not knowing whom to talk to about stopping the changes. They started group after group to try to fight the changes, but those went nowhere. All of the groups they started failed and crashed to the ground as people either gave up and left or saw the advantage of the new city structure.

The other members of my family didn't believe such disabilities were real because they weren't visible. For people who needed one-on-one help, the rest of my family would believe such people needed the accommodations, but for people like me who just needed some help occasionally, they wouldn't think about why we needed help. They just thought it wasn't real. My aunt and uncle were the only ones who didn't share the family belief and would help anyone who had some type of disability, visible or not. I haven't heard from them since I got diagnosed, though, as my parents didn't want them to make me think I had a disability.

I didn't know what to think. The rest of my family despised these changes, though I enjoyed the few I knew of. I never really felt all that different from the people moving into our community, as I had known them my whole life. I grew up adapting to these changes and not noticing them unless I was told. Where my father and mother—

and eventually my brother—felt isolated in the community, I felt isolated by those I lived with.

I hated the view of the world my parents gave me, as it would mean forsaking the friends I had made. Different people talked to my parents about their beliefs and how they were hurting the community. Only accepting part of the community and not all of it hurt others. My parents tried to raise me to use certain words that (after I learned their meaning and what they implied about others) I will not repeat. My aunt and uncle don't know about this, but they often talk and praise our city for starting the changes. My parents will usually get angry after the call, but they hold their tongues around them, so as not to destroy family relations. I don't know what will happen if they come and visit in person.

One of the more significant changes happened when I was around ten years old. Diagnostic testing became mandatory for everyone; it started with elementary students and moved to high school. My parents fought against this test, but eventually, the school convinced them. It was being discussed as a standard, and our school system was a pilot. I took the test; the moderators were helpful and friendly, assisting me when I needed it. I had trouble reading some of the words and took extra-long on them. Sometimes the testers would read the words aloud.

People asked me questions, and then I was taken back to my class, but the people continued to watch me and talk with my teachers. This was done to see how I acted around others in a natural environment like playing. That day, I think I played by myself in my own little world and almost ran into a few of my peers. My teachers had been taking notes about me since I was young, monitoring my behavior, and seeing how I acted. The teachers did this with many students, in preparation for the screening that was now happening.

Eventually, it was discovered that I had ADHD, autism, and dyslexia. People tried to tell my parents about what I had and the help I should receive. My parents refused to let me get help, saying that I wouldn't need it and that I could be "normal." They didn't want to accept that I wasn't like them and that I would be told I needed help for an imaginary problem. My teachers disagreed, but since I didn't have a family meeting for accommodations, there was little they could do for me in terms of offering the same level of accommodations. My parents just ignored this, thinking nothing of it and not offering any help to a problem they didn't view as existing. Many of my teachers disagreed and still gave me support. Since my parents didn't want to get involved, one of our neighbors, Ms. Shelly, stepped up and offered help.

I was glad to get the help, as it made me more like my friends. All of my friends were tested when they were younger, just entering or leaving preschool. Now I am getting help and knowing why I am different and why my parents are always correcting me.

I sometimes wish I hadn't been given help, because when my parents found out, I got a verbal lashing like none before. That talking down also started to change my perspective. I break into tears whenever I think about what they said. I am both grateful and angry that they found out. I didn't need to fear them learning the truth. I was free to stop hiding, but now I was alienated from my family. My father thought I should be like my brother, a normal child. My brother hadn't been tested yet, as he was in high school then, and they started testing in elementary and middle schools. Mother didn't like what I was becoming, although she never outright stated that. Still, it showed through her actions.

The family I had always known didn't want me now. My family hated me because I had accepted accommodations for a problem they thought didn't exist. I didn't know what to do. The assistance I was being given helped me to succeed. I was learning how to speak and how to read with the same skill level as my peers. I was getting help and therapy for speech and reading that I had never gotten before. Life, for me, was degrading, but improving at the same time. I was confused as to what I should do now, seeing two different worlds and being forced to live in both.

I know that I should want my family to love me, but I just don't know what to do. I slowly felt the love for me in the house leave when I had trouble performing with what was viewed as a routine task. I wasn't able to do what they thought I should be able to do; I needed help with some simple tasks. I had trouble mowing the lawn, due to the sound of the mower. So, I didn't get that task. I could cook, but they didn't want to risk me burning myself because I was clumsy. I was left alone in the house with nothing my parents expected me to do.

I felt alone in this terrible life situation. Others around me, my friends and teachers, would try to help, but my family would push them away. I was withdrawing from many of the activities I had been part of previously, and that, according to my parents, just made me behave worse. I was different to them because I was no longer hiding away my stims and hyperactivity from them. Now I became my own person, showing who I was—not my parents' ideal child. This only started after I learned why I had different ideas than my family.

Previously I had done martial arts and different physical activities like rock climbing. These activities were all provided by the school but needed parental permission to do. My parents forced me to stop the activities that helped me. I took comfort talking to my teachers; they attempted to explain what was happening. My parents claimed I was "losing control of myself" and "stopping to function randomly."

One of my teachers' explanations was that it was due to the sudden change in routine, and after I got settled again, it would get better. Another reason was because I didn't have a way to vent my energy and emotions. I was bottling them up and releasing them randomly.

I didn't know what was right, but I tried to be normal at home like my parents wanted. Eventually I was masking my behavior. When I first learned that I was neurodiverse, I didn't hide away what I was, but over time, I started to do so as a means of protection. I would hide what I was told were the stims I had. Stims were my ways of seeking different types of simulation from myself or from the environment. I would try to stop bouncing, needing to focus on preventing myself from performing the habit. Another part I worked on stopping was noisemaking, which, according to my father, "was an embarrassment to be seen around a person acting so differently."

Through speaking with my counselor, I found out that I was masking. I was working to decrease the noticeability of my stims. I forced myself to work through loud noises and bright lights, which was more sensory integration. My stims were mostly hitting and chewing, though I also craved to hear or make certain sounds. I would repeat motions like certain signs, for what seemed to others to be no reason. I would also repeat certain phrases because of how they felt in my mouth, helping me to calm down. I hit my feet together, as it was harder to put pressure on the tops of my feet than the rest of my body, I would also hit my calves with my feet and clap my hands together. I would sometimes chew my lip, though now I was using my chewies more. I was seeking that type of stimulus for some reason. I don't know why; they had just become a habitual part of my life. I don't remember when I started, but I had been doing them as long as I could remember. Most of my friends just ran their hands over different textures or repeated different phrases. I knew people like me who had similar stims, but we were all told to stop, as we were hurting ourselves.

The world continued to change around me—slowly, so it was manageable. I continued to do my best in school, and the help I was getting made me do even better. My teachers eventually stopped telling my parents what was happening at school, only sending home notes, which my parents would rarely read. They would sign permission slips without talking or thinking from what I could tell all I need to do was give it to them and asked nicely.

I was having more and more trouble not masking around those I knew would accept me. My friends were lucky. I don't think they ever felt any pressure to change and to be "normal functioning people," as my father would sometimes say.

I hated what my life had become, being afraid of my family and needing to hide around others so I wouldn't get in trouble. I was given different items to help with sensory issues and remove my harmful stims. Working with my teachers on hitting myself changed to hitting a pile of fabric I had at my desk. Chewing my shirt and lip changed to chewing on what they called a chewie. I was given a few necklaces for this purpose. Luckily, my parents never saw their real purpose; I just told them it was a reward for my hard work. I would be given fidgets that I explained away as toys. I was given options for doing different crafts. My favorite was weaving, and my teachers would hang my projects up around the room.

I loved working with these new people and not being seen as weird. This was great, and it helped make me happy. But any happiness I had would vanish when I would enter my house and need to hideaway. I would spend as many nights as I could at my friends' houses, where I didn't feel the need to hide. I could only do that so often every month before my parents would force me to stay home. I continued to live in two different worlds, and I knew which one I would pick to live in if I had a choice.

# CHAPTER 2

# *Drastic Change*

I HAD BEEN LIVING that life for the past few years, and now my life was about to change. I was moving into high school, and I knew the new school would be a massive shock more so than when I moved into middle school. Having a schedule that continued to change would be a difference I hadn't known before now.

Each school was different but similar. In middle school, I had more classes in a day but more breaks. Now for high school, I had three classes every day for two hours a day. There were two breaks mandated by the school. Apparently, teachers could have multiple breaks or times for students to be able to leave the class without missing too much if they wished to be kind. I was taking six classes total, like in college, just "at a lower level and more often" is how it was described to me. This was a change from the previous schedule, to help us adapt to a college schedule. Previously, according to my brother, the schedule had around seven classes a day plus any band or sports practice before school.

The school I was going to was called Jefferson High, though students often called it AU High School, after the elemental symbol for gold. That was more of a nickname. All the schools in the district were known as special schools; each had a different nickname, depending on what they were designed to best serve. Another high school called Hawkings High was nicknamed Adaptive, working with people who had a physical disability such as not being able to walk. Adaptive High School worked with many more than that, but those are what come to mind. Many classes had combinations of students from the different high schools in the area and even a few nearby middle schools. This is because if they were limited to only one school, the class would not be able to happen. The other reason was because of different facilities the school had like kitchens, a mechanics shop, and others. The schools also had a few college courses for adults to take if they paid the tax for schools. These were some of the compromises made to the different schools to be more accessible.

The area had continued to change and evolve. More teachers were hired with specific education in working with neurodivergent people. Teachers were hired who could work with individuals who had physical differences such as not being able to walk, having a limp, being in a wheelchair, or not having use of an arm, to a name few. These specialized teachers taught both students and older teachers how to work with special populations. Testing for accommodations continued around town, and everyone got tested every three years to see if new disorders or disabilities came up. Revisions of accommodations happened every year.

    I had little change in my test results. I got moved to a program to help me adapt to living and being independent. I learned how to do laundry and cook without getting hurt. (Most students went through courses like this during tenth grade, but I wanted to do them early, so I was taking them.) By this point, I was mostly independent, because of my parents' treatment of me. I wish things were different, but I didn't want my current life to change if that were to happen. I continued to work differently, in similar ways to my peers. Some of our teachers would have trouble with the way we thought. Many teachers were also neurodivergent, so that made learning for them more relaxed, as they could mostly understand how we thought.

    My art teacher showed me this. Most of the art teachers had experience working with different types of people and learning styles. My favorite teacher back then was Mr. David. He introduced me to weaving. One of the main types of changes was how the teachers were qualified to teach. Mr. David was able to work with almost anyone. He could help them to make some form of art by themselves if they could. He had some specific software that could be used to track voice or movement and have that turned into a beautiful drawing, based on movement and tone of voice. Another person would move the audio spectrum around to make an image by recording how it looked at different intervals.

    My parents continued to hate the changes that were happening to what they viewed as their city. They wanted everyone to be able to work under the same standards and refused to accept the accommodations of their coworkers. My family grew to be hated by our neighbors, due to their attitude toward people who were different. I was accepted; I didn't have the same view as my family. I found fellowship with neighbors and grew closer to others.

My neighbors would offer shelter to me and celebrate my accomplishments with me. This was mostly done by my neighbors Neal and Shelly, a sweet older couple who were actually some of my first customers for my drawings and eventually my weavings. They introduced me to the various venues I go to sell my artwork, like churches in the area and a few conventions. Both of their kids are grown and moved out. If I remember what they told me correctly, Mr. David actually went to school with both of their kids back in the day.

By the time I started high school, I had stopped identifying with my family, and we all did our best to ignore each other. We held a mutual hatred for each other. I worked and enjoyed speaking to others who were neuro-atypical, which by this point was a good part of the city. The city became a beacon for what could be done to adapt to work with those who had a variety of disadvantages. Our schools were some of the top-ranked in meeting varying needs of students from different backgrounds, no matter what.

In the almost ten years that I had been going to school, the change was drastic, if you compare the schools before and after. Life had changed for the better, in my opinion, and this was when the changes to my life began—a journey of change and learning a new reality.

# CHAPTER 3

# *Walk to School*

It was a cloudy day in September, a week after my freshman year of high school started. I woke up in my room that I had put together myself. My bed was in the corner next to the window. Under the window was my dresser, as I call it. My dresser was made of six plastic sliding bins holding all of my clothing. These were made in my favorite colors. All in dark colors or darker shades as they didn't hurt my eyes. I hated bright colors, so I used darker shades of the rainbow and cooler colors.

Four bookshelves filled up one wall. Two were full of different types of games. I had painted them to be the same colors as my dresser. Games helped me express my ideas and play with my friends in a contained way that enabled us to learn about each other.

One of the bookshelves was full of different books. The other one had various art and craft supplies. Next to my bookshelves, I had a desk with a few bundles of yarn and fabric scattered around. Most of the books I had were on crafting and showed me how to do different projects. I had a variety of textured books to look through and feel. Sadly, there were few books with characters I identified with. None of the writers I had access to wanted to write about the challenges people like me face. Some of the songs I listen to have similar ideas to what I feel. Some of the therapy I went to had me listen to music to identify the different emotions of the singer. I would listen to many different songs with varying tones and try to figure out the feelings. Books sadly didn't have the tone as easy to see. I liked cartoons; emotions were easy to spot, and I knew what was happening.

I got up and dressed in a set of loose sweatpants and a textured shirt. The textured shirts were gifts from my neighbors, after they noticed I liked the blankets they had made of such material. I then put on my soft socks that were also a gift for starting high school. I went with the light-blue ones. I chose my soft socks, as I could run my toes over them to get sensory. Thinking about that, I should try to get socks made of my shirt material. My toes might rip the fabric, so that might not be the best idea. I could get a lap blanket, I guess, but that wouldn't be the same. I couldn't be discreet at home with it. I put on my coat and left it unzipped; the coat was a dark plaid design with green, blue, and purple for the plaid colors and a black hood.

Choosing to wear my dog-tag chewy, I put it on, along with one of the bracelets I made in occupational therapy. The colors today were a light blue and pastel green to match my socks and shirt. I still go for feeling, but now I have an excellent base on what to wear and get help with. Matching colors used to provide some trouble, as I would go more for feel. I guess I am lucky that my parents haven't noticed the point of my necklaces; some have a company name and logo on them. If they knew the purpose behind these necklaces, they would force me to stop using them and take them away. I don't like chewing on the harder ones; they feel weird and sometimes hurt my teeth. I prefer to use one that are soft and had give, compared to hard rubber ones.

Next, I grabbed my black backpack with texture spots along the straps. I put in the weaving project I had started last night, along with a bundle of yarn. I put my computer, which was given to me by the school to do work on, in my backpack. I also had my sketchbook and a set of colored pencils. Checking the special pocket in my bag, I saw my different sensory tools like my sunglasses, earplugs, a small set of fidgets, some scented items that were sealed away for the moment, and a few more tools. I have many fidgets to use, but my favorites are the moving or textured ones. I have a couple of small stress balls. I have sewed some stress balls in the past that were interesting to make but not my favorite.

I was almost ready to head out to school. I only needed my shoes and food to eat at school. The only meal I ate at home on weekdays now was dinner, so I could spend as little time as possible around my family.

I headed downstairs, hoping my family was still asleep. It was around seven in the morning, and my school started at nine. I left early in the morning, hanging out in one of the craft rooms, either drawing or weaving on a portable loom I had. Looking into the dining room, I realized I wasn't quite that lucky, as my brother was awake; he was home on vacation. Luckily, he would leave our house in a week, though the college he went to was only an hour's drive away. He lived near campus to cut down on gas costs and to be closer to his classes and friends who lived in the area.

"Hello, brother. Hoping to get by on the work of others again this year?" He said more after that, but I am unwilling to repeat the hatred he had for me, as I don't want to remember and bring back memories again. I was hoping he would remain the same as he was at the start of the summer. College had changed him for the better, because he didn't hear any hate from our parents. This is what has happened every summer break since he started college. I'm still holding out hope for him to change for the better; it may be futile, but things could change.

I remained quiet, grabbing one of the breakfast sandwiches I had prepped last night. My family refused to touch them; they didn't want to get sick because they didn't think I could cook. My brother got angry at my ignoring him, but I just continued on my way, leaving him behind, yelling at me. I walked out the door heading to school. It was about a mile away, but I liked the walk. I enjoyed seeing all of the different colors around me. The sun was currently behind cloud cover, so I didn't feel the need for my sunglasses. I saw many people out and about, doing different tasks.

I waved and said hi to many different people. I would sometimes stop for a bit to say hi to those I was friends with or the parents of my friends. This was one of my favorite parts of the day, just being able to walk around with little worry of what would happen. I could forget about my home and be myself. I reached the path that cut through different fields and behind houses leading to my school.

I saw Mr. David heading the opposite way to his job at the elementary school. I am hoping he will come and teach my art class in the future, as he is an excellent teacher. Today we didn't talk, but last year I got to leave my middle school classes to visit and speak to his class about what I do. I talked about the different types of art I do and how I sell what I make around town.

I found this path at the start of middle school, and I loved just wandering around by myself, as it seemed few people remembered the road. I was alone on my walk to school with little fear; I walked this path daily and knew the routes. I also knew many of the people in the houses surrounding the road. This was an enjoyable place to walk, but you needed to pay attention, or you could trip on a root or hit a pothole.

None of the dogs were in the backyards today; I didn't hear any barking of greeting. I usually will get a bark, and then the person in the backyard will say hi. Typically, John and his dog, Duke, are in the backyard playing before John heads off to school.

# CHAPTER 4

# *Old Experience Changed To New*

I CONTINUED MY WALK to school in silence. The wind was a bitter kind of cold but not too unpleasant. I zipped up my coat, pulled up the hood, and continued on the path to school. The sun began to glare in my eyes. I paused, closing my eyes, and fumbled for my sunglasses, I eventually was able to put them on, but a headache had started, and I was beginning to spiral.

    I sat on the cold ground, trying to gain my bearings. I sat in my shadow with my back to the sun, absorbing heat and taking the brunt of the wind. My head began to pound, and I felt myself losing the ability to speak. I sat there waiting to feel better. Normally this happens in my room or a controlled place around others who can help me. *Why couldn't this have waited until I was at school?*

    I sat there on the sidewalk next to the school with my head in my hands and a backpack on my back. Normally I am a happy and energetic person, maybe a little quiet when I get—what is the word?—Oh, anxious, I think it is, Now I'm not moving. I don't know. I don't really feel different, depending on the situation; I just act differently, but I don't notice it. I just stim more and only notice if it is pointed out to me. I am still and in pain, a sharp contrast from my normal personality and how I normally act.

    I sat and waited for this to pass. I didn't know what else to do but wait. Sure, I could have signed something, but no one was around. Even then I could only really do *yes*, *no*, and fingerspelling because I had only one hand free, with the other hand supporting my aching head. My body was curled up to block sensory input, and I was not in the right space of mind in, I only felt a weird type of pain. This is a fear I have of only being able to communicate in one way; normally I can communicate in a couple of ways like spoken and written English along with ASL, but now I can barely do anything.

    I saw shadows pass over me, but I was not noticed, as I was off to the side of the path and many of them were most likely plugged into headphones or talking to others. I wasn't making much noise overall, even though I was in pain. I was alone in my own little world of pain. I don't know how to describe this, except that I couldn't see because of the light but also the darkness. Both hurt, but I don't know which was worse. The light was shining through my eyelids even though they are closed and blocked out.

The wind was bustling around; the sound hurt, but not as much as the light. The chill was manageable thanks to my coat, but it still hurt my head. The wind felt like I was next to a loudspeaker. I was still blank, unable to react to the world.

Normally these passed quickly, but this seemed to be taking longer. I hoped this wasn't one of my hourlong ones. I was taught coping strategies for when these happened, but none of them would help now.

So, I just sat and waited till I felt better, not knowing when that would happen, just hoping I didn't get worse.

Slowly I lifted my head and found the pain had subsided to a manageable level. I stood up shakily and tried to check my phone for the time. The screen was too dark in my sunglasses, so I removed them quickly to see the time before placing them back where they were. This time it was only for a few minutes, luckily. Moving slowly, I continued on to school to keep myself balanced. I grabbed my earplugs from my bag and put them in to try to help.

Entering the school, I felt better because of the setup. I removed my sunglasses but kept my earplugs in. I am allowed my glasses; that doesn't mean I want to wear such noticeable items around. If my parents saw a picture of me in them inside, they would not be happy.

I walked around, heading toward my first class of the day, passing by few people, as the school had just opened to let people in. I continued on my journey, passing the school's mental health section. This was where I will have my counseling session today to modify my stims and talk about why I do them. I continued on to my classroom.

# CHAPTER 5

## *Art With Old but New Teacher*

I HAD FINALLY REACHED my classroom and was ready to go and craft. I had known the teachers at this school for a couple of years, even though this was my first-year attending. Every year, teachers would swap to teach classes in the lower grade level for a week, so they could meet students they would work with soon and know different strategies of teaching through lesson plans and classroom arrangement. This helped to make the transition from school to school and grade to grade easier, as you would already know some of the teachers. Even the principals moved around schools for a week or would swap teacher and principal duties with a teacher so they could remember what it was like in the classroom. So, it was like all the schools had the same large staff. I also meet a lot of the art staff at my art sales; they hear about me from Mr. David and my other art teachers.

I decided to go to my first class of the day, art, which focused on different styles of art. For the course, you were required to make at least a minimum number of projects. You could use the knowledge you already had or do a project the teacher recommended.

To do an outside project, you would need teacher permission and explain how you know the skill, or you could schedule to come before or after class to learn the craft. I got approved to do a variety of weaving and drawing projects. Ms. Brown already knew of my skill in weaving, as I would sell the different pieces I made, to get materials and various games. People often requested me to make different objects and to design different patterns to sew or sculpt. I was well known in the city for my talent with art, and this helped me to make many diverse friends.

My parents didn't care about my skills; they thought I wouldn't be able to make a living off of just art and would fail in life because of my talent and what I focused on. I never told them about selling my art after their first rejection; I didn't want to get hurt again. Everyone I sold to like the work I made and continued to buy from me because of the quality, and my quality continued to improve. I worked hard at what I know to be fun and get enjoyment from. For me, that is the medium of art.

I was about seventy-five minutes early, but Ms. Brown was sitting there calmly in front of the classroom with a broad smile. Entering the room, I had a large smile too.

The lighting system in the school was designed to be soft, to look like the light coming through thick cloud cover, so it didn't overwhelm anyone. This was one of the changes made to the school to improve the comfort of the students. Another change was making it so the noise from other classrooms would be minimal. One of the more recent changes was about every five classrooms, there was a room split into four sections. The sections had controllable lights, sound-canceling walls, and controllable lights that could change color. A desk was in the room for students to do their work if the classroom was too loud.

Similar measures had been implemented in every school in the district. Out-of-district students would come just for the building and level of qualified teachers. I loved the changes and the new way of life in this city, but my family hated it. This was one of the disagreements my family had, over the school and the varying accommodations it made. My family disliked what they didn't consider normal, which included me.

Ms. Brown saw me and signed, *Welcome back, Mark. I am guessing you are here to do some art?* I nodded with a smile. *All right, then how about you go over to your seat and get started. If you need any help, you may raise your hand or come over and get me from my desk.*

I signed back, *will do and thank you.* I headed over to my desk, pulling out from my backpack what I was most recently working on at home. Whenever someone would enter the room, a small buzzer would vibrate to let the hearing-impaired teacher know someone was there if they weren't looking at the door.

I had a fancy collapsible loom made from wood that split into three folding pieces. The loom was unfolded into a one-and-a-half-foot-long by nine-inch-wide object. The weave was already halfway done, using slightly thicker yarn than usual. The weave was of a simple whirlpool image, using a yarn-dyed with multiple colors of blue to make the effect. I also had some paint designed to be used on weaving projects which worked nicely on the yarn I was using. The strands were woven in between, starting out lighter, going from the center to the outer edges. For the edges of the piece, I used different browns on the top to show a landmass, with a few spots of green. I changed between the weave I was doing to create different effects. After the base was done, I was going to do a circle weave and attach it to the top of my current, continuing to make different effects. This was the first time I was attempting a piece like this, and I hoped it would turn out nice.

I continued to weave, practicing my different techniques, as this was an experiment. I used strategically placed stitches to hold the yarn the way I wanted so I could change the look later. The weave was coming together. Looking up, I saw my teacher working hard, drawing something, then pausing and remaking the piece farther down on another piece of paper. There was a stack of paper I could see, and I got curious, so I stopped weaving and went over to ask what she was doing.

Moving over, I stood in front of Ms. Brown and tapped her shoulder. She looked up with a smile. The school taught me how to sign when I was younger so I could communicate; I was considered nonverbal until the age of six. This didn't make my parents happy. They knew I wasn't mute; I could make sounds, just not words. At home, communication didn't really happen between my parents and me. The only way I had of telling them what I wanted was through my teachers and neighbors, who would speak to them for me. I was the odd child out, but after I learned to speak, I was accepted better by my family.

The school saw that I had trouble speaking, so the speech therapist taught me to sign as an alternative means of communication. I was *able* to speak since I was around three or four, but people didn't give me enough time to speak, so I stopped trying unless I was forced. Still, sign is my preferred means of communication, because I hate how people need to ask me to repeat myself multiple times during a conversation. People thought I have an accent, but that was more due to me having a speech delay.

My family trained me to speak correctly, but I have trouble understanding others when I speak the way they want. It gives me a headache, so I rarely speak at home. My family didn't want me to speak with what they viewed as a weird accent. They were okay with me signing, since they hated how my voice sounded. I could communicate fine in sign, but my family didn't want to learn that language for me, since I wasn't deaf or mute.

After all these years, signing just became a habit for me, and it was comforting. Ms. Brown, the art teacher, appreciated my signing. She had hearing loss and used hearing aids; she could verbally communicate and hear but preferred to communicate in sign or with writing. I was similar, but I wanted to work on speaking, so I did, and people appreciated that I had multiple means of communication.

Standing in front of my teacher, I said to her, hoping she would hear me, "What are you working on, Ms. Brown?" I looked over and saw the same drawing in multiple different stages.

Signing back to me, she said, *I am working on showing the different steps of development for one drawing. What do you think?*

Looking over her work, I could see the stages of a person sitting and playing guitar. The different development stages she went through before the final version she was working on were scattered around.

I decided I should just sign, as speaking was hurting my head slightly. *Those look very nice. I am excited to see what you will do in the class. Are we moving on to doing some animation?*

*No, we are not moving on to doing animation just yet. I am glad that you like how this looks. Do you think I could see your weaving right now?*

I smiled at her and signed back *yes* before going to grab what I had been working on. The weave was almost done, and I was about ready to start on the second half of the project.

*That looks very nice. I hope you will be able to finish it soon so I can see the finished project. Look at the time. Class is about to start. Now let us go and get ready for class.*

Moving back to my desk, I put away my project, went over to the student cabinet, and pulled out the weaving activity I was doing for the class.

I was working on doing a multilayer weave to try to recreate the look of hills with weaving and careful placement. This would be a 3-D piece of artwork, and I had only just finished a few of the hills. I still had a lot of work left on this project, but luckily, I had ninety minutes. Every day we had three classes split into one-and-a-half-hour blocks with an hour lunch break period and two fifteen-minute break passing period things. I started on weaving another one of my hills out of green and brown fabric, rarely changing the type of weave.

Weaving was one of the actions that I was redirected to do whenever I would start hitting my hand on the desk to get movement. I can pay attention to the class and my weave at the same time, so that is fun. My family was happy that I was quiet in my activities. I was left alone, as most of my first art supplies came from excess from the classroom, mostly from Mr. David, and also from Neil and Shelly.

My classmates started to pour into the classroom, some with headphones on, some with hearing aids, some with sunglasses, some with gloves, some with chewies in mouths like the one I had on my neck, and many more items to help them function. Everyone was different and had some way to cope or help function in the classroom. The other art teacher entered the classroom; this was the speaking teacher who worked mostly with the hearing and speaking students, though he did know some basic sign language.

All teachers, by this point, were required to have a way to teach the nonhearing or nonspeaking students. Many of the subjects had two teachers to help educate both sides, and many other students knew sign language because of how many students used it. I loved this adaptation; it meant I could speak to an adult in sign language regularly outside of therapy. Not speaking became normal for the school, as many students couldn't communicate verbally or could only say a few words. I loved the changes the area has gone through; now there are people I easily relate to and can speak with about the experiences I have had.

I continued to do one of my favorite activities that I could focus entirely on and never get bored, weaving. I loved the feeling of the yarn on my finger, and the sense of creating something that can be used is unbeatable. The class continued on with us either learning new ways of drawing from the teachers or working on different projects.

When the time came for the class to change, the lights dimmed considerably for a few seconds before returning to normal levels. It was time class was over.

# CHAPTER 6

## *Break to Prevent Overload*

It was time for one of the breaks of the day. The courtyard happened to be nice today and had plenty of seating. Early on, I learned that many people happened to congregate to the courtyard during breaks and lunch. Normally I would be in the art room if I was in middle school. This year I wanted to make a few new friends.

Walking to the courtyard, I could see a few people tossing around a football. Many were sitting at the tables, though a lot were on the ground. A group were playing soccer in the nearby field. The field was giant and filled with chaos everywhere; many people were ducking, afraid of being hit on the head. Light reflected off of all the bright clothing and reflective pieces. I heard a lot of yelling as people played games, growing in sound as time moved on. I was afraid I would get hit on the head. Balls and gossip flew around, along with some food when the tables got bumped. Slowly backing away to return into the building, I almost ran into the person behind me due to my haste.

"Hey, are you okay?"

I started to sign; I couldn't speak right now. *Help.*

*My name is Steve. What do you need help with?*

*Loud and bright.*

*Okay, follow me.*

I followed behind Steve, remembering that he is one of the helpers of the school. He helps people with sensory problems move to the sensory areas of the school. There are many people like Steve in the school, though luckily, I never have needed their help this term, until now. I used their help in my previous schools, but I had managed until now. These people are like the ones who know about a person having diabetes and help them with blood sugar level. Instead of helping with my blood sugar, they help with sensory problems. Many helpers like this are in the school, each one doing a different task, like those for allergies, sensory, diabetes, and many more different problems.

I followed Steve. We reached a nearby room and went inside. Steve turned down the lights, and I sat down. Turning my backpack around, I pulled out my sunglasses and put them on. Luckily, I had gotten away before it became overwhelming and didn't go into sensory overload. Normally it was harder to leave such a situation, but Steve helped me a good amount.

*I'm doing better. Thank you for the help. I think I am good.* I truly was feeling better, though not the best, as I was still recovering. The signing was helping, along with the lowered lights and quiet environment.

*Good. would you like me to walk you to class?* He had a smile on his face as he asked me.

Feeling up to speaking now, I said, "Sure, Steve. How are you doing?"

"I am doing good, Mark; that is your name, correct?" Steve was looking at me again, next to my face, not at my eyes, which was more comfortable.

Putting out my hand for a handshake, I said, "You are correct. My name is Mark. Thanks for the help." Before the school year, students could sign up for different students hired by the school, like Steve and professional teachers and staff, to know who we are in case we need help, though it is all confidential. The school would hire different students for different jobs where peers might be more helpful compared to staff. The helpers would know how to work with those in or nearing sensory overload and how to help them not get more overwhelmed.

"You're welcome." Looking down at his watch, Steve continued, "We should probably start heading to class."

"Okay, let's head out." Both of us walked out of the room. I felt better than I was earlier.

"What are you doing this weekend, Mark?"

The walk was nice, and I was excited to answer, hoping to see him at my art sale. "I am doing an art sale at the church on Twenty-Fourth Street. You are welcome to come." I tried my best to smile at him. I wanted to see him there so I could introduce my new friend to my friends Kyle and Sarah. I have science with Steve, I think. We don't have assigned seats, so if I see him, I will attempt to sit next to him.

Normally I am in my own little world, shut off from those around me, but I was trying to make new friends. I was hoping that

I made a friend with Steve, instead of making a new friend in the courtyard.

"I will try, but I might have homework. If you like, we could exchange phone numbers." Steve turned to me, and we stopped in the mostly empty hallway.

"Sure," I said, reaching, for my phone so we could exchange numbers. Afterward, we continued on to the gym. Steve walked me to the changing room door before heading off. We exchanged pleasant conversation the whole way to the gym.

# CHAPTER 7

# *Martial Arts for Gym*

The class I had after art was physical education. The exciting thing about PE was you could select one of three choices for what to do during the period. Option one was practicing different forms of dance and doing yoga. Option two was doing martial arts. The version offered was mostly a self-defense class, so more mixed martial arts. The class did have three teachers, each a master of multiple styles of martial arts. The third option was to play and learn about different types of sports.

I went with the martial arts option. The main options were Jujitsu, Tae Kwon Do, and Tai Chi. My counselors signed me up for the tai chi option to help me learn patience outside of weaving.

One thing stayed the same with all of PE: we would all go to track, either indoor or outdoor, and either walk or run for thirty minutes, whatever we felt up to on that day. Due to the nature of the martial arts class, we mostly copied the movements of the teacher, though there was an interpreter also with each of the instructors who had only basic knowledge of the topic.

The other piece was we were expected to wear clothing we could work out in without problems. Many people had separate clothing for this class, but many just wore the same style of clothing for the whole day. The locker rooms were designed to offer safety and comfort to everyone. That is why there are changing cubicles like the ones at clothing stores for the students to use if they wanted.

It was now time to go out and do our walking/running activity. I loved this; we only had to do what we had the energy for and could go at any speed we needed, as long as we attempted the activity.

The teachers were accommodating, demonstrating the different moves and then having us repeat until we were able to replicate the form with little problem. This was amazing; the teacher was very patient and would go around helping every student to improve. There were few problems, if any. If a person felt anger, they were more than welcome to go and run on the track or to take out the frustration on the training dummies in the room.

As far as I knew, almost everyone enjoyed PE, due to the number of options for classes people could choose from. The exercises were fun, and some were even designed to help lower energy levels of some students like myself. Multiple sets of exercises were available for us to use, so we could pick our favorite one to do before moving on with the rest of the lesson.

While I love being able to move and exercise, I did have some problems with the class. Many times, we would be sent outside, and construction would be happening nearby, preventing me from doing the whole track, or the sun would shine right in my eyes, making it hard to run. I loved to run; I could move so fast and free and just forget the world, entering my own reality while I walked around.

My parents hated when I did this in public; they viewed me speaking to myself or swinging my arms as embarrassing. My brother, for all his faults, didn't really care, as long as I didn't hit him.

At school and away from the people I lived with, I could be myself without hiding or feeling hatred. I disliked having to put on a mask, but it was a means of survival. The way to live in that home was to pretend you could function correctly without help, and the life you would get would be one of love and happiness. Though if a person were like me and needed help, they would only receive hate for their difference.

I continued in the class, though my thoughts were not on what was happening. I could barely focus, so I just went through the movements and continued to practice letting my mind wander.

The exercise continued, and now we were on the part where we just needed to repeat the forms and continue with the actions, to help strengthen those parts of the body and build memory. During the continued repetition, the lights began to dim and brighten again. The part that was different about the school's gym was the lights dimmed five minutes before the rest of the school, to give time to change. The electronic locks on the locker room would stop and let students in to change.

# CHAPTER 8

## *Counseling With Old Ally*

ON FRIDAYS, DURING MY lunch, I would schedule my counseling appointments. This was where I would work to improve my stims and get less nervous about spending time at home. My counselor was Jaden; he would change schools every day to work with more students. He was amazing and has worked with me since I was diagnosed by the school.

Some of our appointments were us just sitting around and talking about random things. Normally, I would talk about different weaving and games I played. He would reply with different ways what I talked about could help me—like how I could chew on my chewies more instead of my lip if I felt—frustrated, I think he called the emotion. Another suggestion was to use a punching bag or to use deep breathing and other exercises I learned in martial arts to adapt and not hurt myself. He is the reason I have a good pair of sunglasses; he recommended that I get them and gave me a coupon they got for stim items such as sunglasses. He also gives me challenges to do with my art.

Jaden was part of the reason I was working on figuring out how to do a 3-D weave. He challenged me to use a different form that normally isn't multilayer and to make it multilayer. I decided to do my weaving, and the challenge I was given moved to the back burner but is going nicely, and I use it to figure out different mistakes in my technique.

I entered the waiting area for the secretaries and stood in the line to wait to check in. The area was big but felt small and cozy. A few plants covered the area, with chairs next to them. A few people were ahead of me, but that was normal for this time. Many students did counseling during lunch when they didn't have classes and could, if they wished, continue after school, unlike if they had an after-school appointment.

The person at the front desk began to talk. "Next in line, please come forward." I walked forward to the front desk to sign in for my appointment. "What is your name?"

"Mark." I had a smile on my face, but I only knew Jaden at this counseling center.

"Nice to meet you, Mark. Do you have insurance?" Many students do counseling here, and their insurance pays for it. It is easier and more convenient for many to go to counseling services on campus than elsewhere. I held out my student ID, hoping she would know what that means. I am under the school district for my counseling. My parents don't want to pay for a service they don't think I need. Luckily, I qualified for the school to cover the cost of my counseling.

"All right, Mark, head on over to the counseling area, and you will be called when they are ready."

I nodded and moved over to sit. Pulling out my small weaving project from my pocket, I got started.

"Mark, it's good to see you. Let's head on up." Jaden was calling my name to go for counseling. I stood up and joined him, walking back. "How are you doing, Mark?"

"I am good, how about you?"

"Good." By this point, we had reached the sealed area and were heading back into the room. We were walking in relative silence; just breathing and our feet hitting the ground was the only sound. When we reached Jaden's room at this clinic, he started to talk again. "Anything new to talk about since we talked? I noticed you didn't call the help line this summer. So, are you doing better?"

"I guess you could say that. My brother came home for the summer, though he will be moving out soon." I had a sad smile at that thought; I wanted him to return to how he was at the beginning of the summer. I wanted Josh to be kind and accepting of me again. Over the summer, he moved more to my parents' philosophy on disabilities than the one he learned at college. I preferred how he acted after he returned from college to how he was at the end of the summer. Josh would take me to different places, and we would talk about what we liked to do, though I never brought up the fact that I sold my artwork.

By this point, we had reached his room. The door was covered in artwork and letters from his clients. Opening the door, he said, "Come on in. Pick a place to sit."

I looked around to see his new room. It was covered in drawings and letters. I could recognize a few of the ones I had made for him on the wall. He had my image of a mountain surrounded by mist with a few trees at the bottom leading and thinning out as the mountain continued up. Another piece was of the two of us at one of the art fairs. This was drawn from how I think we looked goofy. He knew I was nervous about that day, so he dressed in a normal outfit that I found funny on him. He had brought me a set of colorfully but deliberately poorly wrapped coloring supplies with some different yarn. This was a present from the school for helping out in all the different classes I had over the year.

"All right, Mark, let's get started with this. So, would you like to talk about your brother, continue working on stims, or possibly your family?" Jaden had a smile on his face, which I think he meant to be kind. He cared for me and offered me support about my family.

"I think a combination of stims and my brother would be good. What do you think?" When I was younger, I liked others to tell me what to do, and I still prefer to ask others to help me to make choices. I ask for advice every time I make what I view as a decision I could be judged on.

"Okay, will do, Mark. Now, how are you feeling?" Jaden was looking at me, not at my eyes but in my direction, which was comfortable. I dislike looking others in the eye, but sometimes I feel the need to.

"I don't know. I guess good? Been stimming more, so I don't know what I am feeling." Stims were a way I took out my anger, nervousness, excitement, and most of my emotions. Some people who know me well can tell my mood based on the stim I do or how I am talking. One example is if I talk fast and excitedly, that means I am tired.

"Okay, could you tell me what type of stim you have been doing? You don't need to tell me, but it could help with how you are doing." Jaden was always nice and didn't try to force me to share information I had trouble with—unlike my family.

"I think I have been chewing my lip more, and I have been hitting myself."

"If I remember correctly, we determined that those relate to nervousness and anger. Though it may also be the fact that you need to ground yourself more than normal."

Shifting back in forth, I didn't know what I should say, as that was true. I had been fighting off a headache and had been more sensitive to stimuli from the environment. "That is a possibility." I paused to think. I knew what I should do. I will tell him; he has helped me in the past with this stuff. "Would having headaches have anything to do with that?"

"Yes, that could impact it. You may be trying to distract yourself from that pain with other pain, as you have done in the past. Have your headaches decreased since starting school, or have they grown? I know you are doing martial arts this year, and I remember that doing such physical activity helped you."

"Headaches have decreased but are still there."

"Okay, maybe talk to your teachers about working with them after school. I'll also talk with them if you'd like, but you asking would also help." The teachers and counselors worked together to help improve the conditions of students if the students gave permission to share what was talked about. I did that with specific teachers, and it has helped me immensely. "Are you still using your chewies and the fabric pile to hit instead of yourself?"

"Yes, sometimes, but it's hard. It's a habit that I don't know how to break." I freaked out some of my friends with my different stims, and I didn't want that to happen as often.

"Remember, Mark, these are normal. You are doing the best you can; it will take time. We only started on such drastic transitions in the past couple of years. These are just ways to not be as harmful and to help you adjust to the world. Remember, these are normal and don't need to stop. To you, these actions are normal; you just want to not cause pain to yourself and others. You shouldn't want to stop stimming. It is a part of you, and I don't want to see how you will change if you lose such a part."

"Okay, Jaden. Could we move on to my brother?" I was getting tired of this talk. I knew I needed it, but I didn't like to hear it. I knew my parents were wrong, but they drilled that idea into my head—the idea that stimming is wrong and needs to be stopped and shouldn't exist. I didn't know how to get such an ingrained idea out of my head.

"Sure, if that's what you want, Mark." I nodded to his statement. "So, what do you want to talk about with your brother? Has he shifted worse this year, compared to the first year?"

"I guess you could say that. He is still better than he was before he went off to college. I just miss how he was at the start of the summer where he was nice and accepted me. He would take me to different places, but then he would slowly revert to how he was in the past, just not as cruel. He would be nice to others and accepting of others' differences, but to mine he would be hateful. This cycle would continue every year, and I would gain hope that he would remain supportive of me, but he would always go back to thinking my problems weren't real."

"How does that make you feel? If you can say, if not, we can just talk." Jaden had what I think was a kind look on his face and a gentle voice as the topic continued. He was nice to me and offered help whenever he could and wouldn't push me unless I agreed or asked.

"I don't know. I am just annoyed and sad. I wish I had my nice brother back." I remembered all the drawings I had made; I teared up and curled into a ball on the big, soft chair. I missed my brother, and I hated what he had become. Though I guessed I should be strong, or else I would fall apart. I took many deep breaths and shifted until I was mostly uncurled, but both feet were still off the ground, supported by the chair. The pressure of gravity pushing my legs into the chair helped.

Jaden smiled, and we just sat there, me lost in thought, knowing if I started to overload, Jaden was there to help me. The lights began to fade, and it was time for me to leave. Jaden helped me more than I think he knew that day, just letting me get lost in thought—though that often happens.

# CHAPTER 9

## *English With New Spin*

IT WAS TIME FOR my final class of the day, English. This wasn't my favorite subject, because of all of the different grammar and spelling rules I needed to follow. I had dyslexia and would mix up letters for numbers sometimes or would misunderstand the writings I read; it was annoying. I worked hard in this class but frequently had trouble.

I worked better with art, where I could feel or see it develop, not needing to imagine what was happening, like when I am writing or reading. For my weaving, I usually drew a pattern or style or took an example of a piece to know what to make. I worked hard at my craft, as I could see the development and change a pattern or understand what went wrong for the future.

I was able to use others' examples of scenery to make crafts or use the descriptions and pictures I was given to make art. The way of viewing the world for me is like I can touch what I make. I don't like others to have the power to make what they want out of what I make. I like to control the interpretation of my work as much as possible. When trying to paint a picture in my writing, I frequently go over it in detail, to the point where it brings down my writing.

Oftentimes, when we are told to write stories, I try to take the first-person point of view because it is easier to only know what one person will say and think. When I try to have the thoughts of many others in the story, I have trouble. When drawing a story, I have a much easier time. I show actions through images and scenery with the accuracy I want. I don't need to show thought unless I wish, and I can show how it looks from just one person looking out.

I mostly see people do drawing like a person is watching without intervening. Most stories are from the third person, so the art doesn't have the point of view of a single character. I dislike stories like this, as it makes it harder for me to imagine what is happening.

Often, people look over the writing I have done and offer advice. When I ask what they mean, frequently no example of the change is given, or the example only applies rarely. The trouble is in keeping all of the different rules straight. Mix-ups often happen, and this confuses others.

In my drawings, at least the people who have seen them rarely get confused. A couple of teachers have asked me to illustrate different social situations to use with students. Doing the illustrations for others also helps me to understand the different situations. Learning in a way that I can be creative is a favorite way of mine. Taking classes with others to learn and interact also helps with learning to socialize.

My English teacher, Mr. Cameron as he liked to be called, tried to make the class enjoyable. He would introduce different topics and short stories. Often, he would have two separate assignments and sometimes even more for us to work on. Letting students chose between reading a novel or a collection of short stories was nice. Both covered the same genre and used similar conventions. The task the whole class had was to compare different writing strategies that were used with the types of stories and how they told different but related stories.

The final assignment, when the class finished reading the type of material they chose, was to do a project. It could be creative or written. Different kinds of tasks would be allowed for the class. This quarter, the class would focus on making creative pieces. A person could write an untold part of the story. For the people who did the short story, they could try to incorporate one of the other characters into a different short story. The people who did the novel, if they wished, they could do this also; they would just need to offer up a story they know and have that option approved.

The option I went with was doing an art piece. I usually did the short story parts, so I would take similar elements of the stories and do a bit of artwork representing the pieces. A person could also write a song or poem about the stories. This class was great and had so many options for the students to do and explore.

What we were graded on was explaining the choices we made and the reason behind those choices. This could either be explained verbally or in writing, depending on student preference. This class was unique; instead of the normal two teachers, it had three.

I mostly worked with Mr. Cameron, since he worked with the more creative-focused students who had trouble picturing what some stories tried to tell. He supported my artwork and even helped give me ideas and talk through what I wanted to do. I had trouble writing down my thoughts, but I could talk about them for hours. So, I scheduled to meet with him, where we would discuss, and he would help record some of my ideas.

The current genre we were exploring was fiction. We were focusing on realistic fiction, different places or societies that could possibly exist in our world; a study of how different people can interpret the same world when growing up different.

The main focus was on similarities. Many of the stories had an aspect of dystopia or utopia. Sometimes the pieces we read would be excerpts from novels. If a student liked the short story, they could decide to stop with the short story route and read the full novel instead. This course was made to work with many different types of readers. The English department was the largest department in the school, though the physical and language programs also made up substantial parts of the staff.

The current class focused on Mr. Cameron and some other students reading the short stories aloud. Instead of taking notes, I would do small drawings of the essential parts of the story to remember. This was a strategy that my previous teachers came up with to help me remember plot points or similar parts between stories. Frequently, the teachers would ask me to show my drawings to my classmates to help them, and I was happy to share my work with others.

I loved to hear people tell stories and just let myself get absorbed by the story and draw on instinct. The pieces I did during this time didn't look bad per se but didn't look the best either, in my opinion. I just continued to draw while listening to the short story.

Before I knew it, the lights were dimming, and the school day was over. I had a fun day overall and was excited for the weekend, as I would be staying with Dr. Joe and going to sell my crafts and drawings.

# CHAPTER 10

# *Home to Brother*

THE SCHOOL DAY WAS over, and it was time to head home. I needed to head back right after school, so I could grab the art material I had left behind when leaving for school. I needed to do this before going over to Dr. Joe's house. I was told to call him when I was on my way.

He is the father of my friends Kyle and Sarah. I frequently stay over at their house before going with them to different fairs.

Tomorrow was the start of a sale at one of the local churches. I got permission to set up a booth to sell my weavings and drawings. Usually the funds raised would go to the church, but we had a deal where we split the profits.

The dinner at Dr. Joe's house started around 6:00 p.m., and school got out at three. I still had some projects left to finish for sale, so I needed to hurry to grab the materials and rush over to their house. I had become fast friends with them when I was younger. I don't actually remember when we first met; I just know I've known them as long as I had been doing art. Dr. Joe helped me with the paperwork for the sales, so I basically had a small business in the city and surrounding area.

I love to craft, and by selling the completed works, I was able to do more art and get clothing and materials I wanted. It was a cycle that, in my mind, everyone benefited from. I would sometimes even do new drawings at the fair if a person wanted to watch. The drawings would always be small, but it helped to give me practice.

I reached my house. It was time to head in and face my brother and possibly one of my parents. Generally, after school, no one would be home, and I could just hurry in and leave after locking the door and have no problem. Though now that my brother was visiting, he usually hung out at home and tried to have a conversation I didn't want to have. I opened the door and was prepared for whatever could be said.

"Hello, brother of mine. Did you get a lot of help today from others?" His tone sounded like what I was told was mocking, though I had trouble telling. I just walked by, ignoring him and not responding. This had become part of the normal routine in the house by this point. I hadn't known any differently in many months, and I most likely wouldn't for more than six months. The only change happened at the start of the year, when he returned home from college, but by now, even if my brother didn't want to act this way, it was a habit he had trouble breaking. He didn't act this way around others, only me, as that was what he knew.

I saw how other families acted around each other, but I knew that we would never be like that. I made a group of friends, and at least to me, they had become a pseudo-family.

I continued upstairs into my room. The TV was playing in the background on some news station, I think. Even though I was now upstairs, I could still hear the show playing. I forgot to put in my earplugs before I came home. I had a set of shooting-grade earplugs to help me when the world was too loud.

Entering my room, I headed over to my desk and grabbed my binders. I had two binders with drawings in them to sell. I also grabbed my artwork cylinder that held some of my larger pieces that didn't fit in my binder, placing them on my desk. I headed over to my bookcase and pulled out a duffel bag.

The bag was a mixture of dark colors, forming a tie-dye pattern. I actually colored in different bags for people for a price. Though for many of my friends, all that was exchanged was the ability to come and stay over more often. I had many different fabric markers and paints to use for designing bags. Putting the design on the bag actually could be very difficult, depending on the bag and the requested pattern.

I grabbed my completed sewing projects to go into the bottom of the bag. I had sewn some bags, purses, shirts, lap blankets, and hats for the craft show. I then grabbed my binders and put them into the bag on top of the sewing. Finally, I grabbed my different weaving projects. I put them into the bag on top of the drawings to create some protection for the binders.

My weaving projects for this time were mostly wall hangings and patterned potholders. I did have an elaborate woven 3-D piece that someone had ordered to be picked up at the fair tomorrow. This piece took me a couple of months, but it looked beautiful. The effect was made by stacking different-sized woven potholder-style pieces together and sewing them together. In the center, I used some foam to add structure, but it was mostly yarn stacked onto itself.

The piece was a cliffside with a waterfall falling down. I made trees sewn onto different foam cores, and for the cliff, I had a backing of cardboard. I had many small weaves to create the look of crashing and rippling water. This was a large piece, and it almost didn't fit into my bag. The piece was two and a half feet wide and three feet long. I had many of the pieces be removable to help with transportation; I would finish attaching them when the client arrived.

For my drawings, I only made a few copies of each that would be considered original, with my signature on them. This time, I mostly had different sceneries for people to buy, but I also had character drawings for people to look at. I was slowly making a graphic novel, and the characters I had for people to buy were scrapped ideas that I had drawn but decided against going into the novel.

The unique thing about the novel was that I worked with one of my friends to make a storyline and the different characters. I would make the graphic parts, and they would write down the non-drawn version of the story. I loved to draw, and this was one of my longest projects. The first book was nearing completion. The main reason we were writing two versions of the same story was for people who had trouble reading when images were involved.

Valentine was helpful with writing the story, as they gave the point of view of a deaf person and understood what would and wouldn't work for the story. In the story, we had characters signing, and I would draw out each panel to show the signs so they were as accurate as I could make them. Valentine was a close friend who helped me with my artwork; they were in college and had more practice. According to them, I was still the better artist. We would both help each other with learning and communicating in sign language; that was our means of communication. Or we could write down our conversations, but why would we do that when we could use sign?

I had all of my artwork packed and ready. Now I just needed to get my clothes ready. I grabbed a second smaller duffel bag and began to put in clothing. I was staying until Sunday evening, so I needed two sets of sleep clothes and two sets of day clothes. I put them all into my bag. Now all I had to do was select which type of socks I wanted. I had three main types, compression, traditional, and soft fluffy. I decided to grab two pairs of compression and two pairs of fluffy socks. I then went and grabbed two of my chewies to wear, along with a small choker, like a necklace with two sides, each one having a different texture.

I put on the textured choker like a necklace and packed the other chewies. I then went and grabbed a second fidget bracelet that had some beads to spin. I had my second duffel bag all ready and set out to leave.

I headed down the stairs with my two duffel bags and my school backpack, so I could work on homework. My clothing duffel was hanging off my shoulder by a strap. My other duffel had wheels on it, so I was rolling the heavier bag. Luckily, Dr. Joe's house was nearby, so I wouldn't need to walk all that far. I had reached the area where my brother was sitting, and he began to speak. "Where are you heading, Mark? To one of your friends' houses? How long are you staying with all of those bags you have?" He had a weird look on his face. This was the first time he had been around when I was heading out to sell my artwork, so he had never seen my art duffel bags. I began to sign back to him, as I didn't want to speak.

*Going to a friend's house.* Before I could finish signing, he interrupted, demanding I write down what I wanted to say or speak aloud. I pulled out my phone, which had a text-to-speech app. I didn't want to write it down; I had a headache coming on. Even though I didn't want to respond, I knew I should, otherwise my father would be angry, and my mother would be upset. They still didn't like it when I didn't speak, but in their minds, it was at least better than speaking in a different language than them.

The app began to speak for me. "I am going to a friend's house for the weekend. I will be back on Sunday."

"What are you doing there with all of this? Is this how much you can't function that you need so much stuff to even function?"

"No. The larger bag is full of different drawings and art I made to sell at the fair tomorrow." I told him that by accident, as I forgot who I was speaking to. After I told my parents about how I liked to do art and they said it would never turn into a job, I stopped telling them about selling art.

My brother had left right around the time I started to visit different events to sell. Now that I think about it, this might be his first-time hearing about this.

"Okay, where are you doing the selling? I want to see how you do and if this is a way for you to make a life for yourself. You'll still be relying upon others' hard work and charity."

"I am doing it at the church on Twenty-Fourth Street. I need to head out. I will see you if you come." I then left the room and headed out the door to Dr. Joe's house.

# CHAPTER 11

## *Walk Away to Real Home*

I USUALLY ENJOY WALKING out of the house and going to see one of my friends. Though now, I was feeling something confusing. I think there was interest about what was happening in my life from my brother outside of the beginning of summer. After those I lived with learned about the accommodations I was getting, acceptance for me was gone. I had turned into a person who needed help for an "imaginary problem," and in their eyes, that was unacceptable. That had been my shut-off from those I lived with.

So how should this change be viewed? My brother, who acted so much like my parents to me, seemed to open up. Interest from a person I was related to who wanted to see my way of work. I was nervous about him seeing my art. When I first showed my parents, they demeaned it as unworthy and essentially trash that wasn't good enough to sell. From then on, I mostly hid and didn't speak about my hobby. Others enjoyed the work and bought the pieces, but my brother—what would he say?

Walking down the sidewalk had been slow so far. Caught up in my thoughts, I forgot about the time I needed to get to Dr. Joe's house. I continued on the now-familiar path to his home. Walking this path so often, memories flooded my mind. I remembered the first time I headed down to his house, when I was around nine. Kyle had given me a map to his house, even though it was only few blocks over, along with directions. At first, I was confused, but the instructions were clear, and I had a map, so I got to their home safely.

While I was reminiscing about my first journey, I continued to walk. I would dodge the occasional sprinkler, as had become a habit. Most families lived on a schedule, and as the children of the family grew older, the schedule would start to relax. Kyle and Sarah lived in an area with many younger kids who had just moved in. Many houses were either recently built or remodeled in this area. I don't know exactly what had changed, as I hadn't visited this section of my neighborhood until I became friends with people who lived in the newer areas.

Luckily, by this point, I had built up some muscles from carrying around different projects and doing martial arts. To some, the bags I carried were heavy, but to me, the pressure and resistance they gave had a calming effect. Something early on I noticed was that I liked pressure or weight to be put on me, like many of my other classmates.

I had compression shirts at home that I would sometimes wear when I didn't want to be in my soft, loose clothing.

Walking around while carrying different bags had become normal for the city. From what I was told, many of the different families would look out for me and try to provide some kind of safety net for the wandering I did alone. Often, other parents or older students would join me on my walks when I was younger. This happened until my thirteenth birthday, but people would still join me on walks, though now it wasn't just to make sure I was safe.

This time, no one joined me on the walk. By this point, because I often walked to people's houses in the area, those living here had begun to recognize me. Most people who lived here for more than a few months had come to recognize who I was.

I was nearing Dr. Joe's house, and all I needed to do was turn at the upcoming park, and his home would be on my right. I walked up the sidewalk until I was standing on their driveway. I went and knocked on the door and waited for them to answer. Kyle was the one to answer the door, and I could smell that dinner was almost ready.

"Hey, Mark, I'm glad you made it. Dad is just finishing dinner. If you want for tonight, you can stay in my room or the guest room. Another option that was given is all of us doing a sleepover in the family room." I had made it, and it was time for dinner and then to set up.

# CHAPTER 12

## *Art With Friends*

ENTERING THE HOUSE, I smelled spices in the air; it seemed Dr. Joe had made a curry. The house had an entrance hall, branching off into the kitchen and the living room, with the dining room attached to the kitchen, making a type of square with the library next to the living room. Along the walls were pictures of Kyle and Sarah at different ages, mostly with other friends. I featured heavily in a couple of them.

"Hello, Mark, how are you doing?" Dr. Joe popped out of the kitchen, giving a quick greeting.

"I am doing good, Dr. Joe. How are you doing?" I was curious, as it had been a few weeks since I had talked to Dr. Joe, and he had a stressful job sometimes. He was one of the people trained to be a counselor for all age ranges and was an emergency counselor for the school system.

"Thanks for asking. I am a little tired but otherwise fine. How about you go and wash up while I finish dinner." Then, turning to Kyle, he said, "After you wash hands, it's your turn to set the table for dinner, Kyle. We will need spoons and the heatproof bowls." Nodding, we both walked off to the small bathroom in the hallway next to the entrance. Kyle washed his hands first. He didn't wait for the water to warm up, just washed his hands with the cold tap water. Then he went to the table. I walked in and turned on the water, waiting for it to get to a comfortable warm temperature before washing my hands with their unscented soap. I walked out to the table and saw Sarah already sitting at the table while Kyle put out bowls and spoons.

"Mark, are you excited for dinner? Dad made a few different types of curry, mostly mild beef and spicy chicken, along with a vegetarian tofu curry that is savory."

Deciding I wanted to sign tonight for the most part, I signed, *Yes, I am. How about you?* I was able to relax here. I knew they understood sign; they had taken the class and also learned from me.

*Would you like for us to sign with you, Mark?* Kyle signed. I was sitting opposite Kyle and Sarah for dinner so we could all see each other.

*If you would like. I don't care either way, but it would be easier for me to communicate.* Kyle and Sarah smiled, the first couple of minutes was catching up on how we were doing. I loved using sign; I could convey so much, and it didn't hurt my head by talking. Sign language let me communicate in a way I wanted, though I also knew I would need to get comfortable at speaking by some point. But for now, I didn't.

Sarah joined the conversation as we were waiting for food. *So, what art do you have for us?* I know Sarah liked more disaster and action type art. She was energetic and quick moving, rarely staying still for more than a few moments.

*I have a drawing of a wolf on a hunt. I think you might like that.*

*I do like that idea. I can't wait to see it.* Sarah had a big smile on her face when she signed that back to me.

*I am excited also. What do you have for me?* Kyle normally waited for me to tell, but I guess he got excited.

*I have an image with your tree and a family of deer in textile.* I had worked on sewing this for a few days, as I knew Kyle would like such a tapestry to go in his room.

*That sounds great. How big is it?* Kyle asked, tilting his head.

*It is around one foot by two feet.* Footsteps entered the room, and we stopped signing. It was Dr. Joe carrying a pot of food. He set it down on the table with a smile before bringing up his hands.

*So, based on the quietness, I am guessing we are using sign tonight.* Dr. Joe was very perceptive and was happy when his kids would practice sign language. It meant they were learning to accommodate and use a second language.

The three of us signed *yes*.

*All right, then, let's eat, and then we can discuss tonight's plans.*

I got a mixture of the tofu and beef curry for dinner. Sarah got the spicy chicken curry with a little tofu. Kyle got beef curry with some cream. Dr. Joe got a mixture of all three. Dinner passed quickly, and we moved on to discussing before Kyle, Sarah, and I went to bed.

*So, where are you going to sleep tonight, Mark?* Kyle asked. Normally, it would change, depending on the sibling and how people were feeling on that day.

*That depends on you and Sarah.* Dr. Joe always gave the choice to his kids if he could, so they could learn how to be independent.

*Could we do a sleepover?* Sarah asked, looking at Dr. Joe with a smile on her face.

*I would like to do that as well.* Kyle was slower and clearer in his signs than Sarah.

*Okay, if Mark agrees, you can, but you will need to clean up in the morning.* Dr. Joe had a smile on his face.

I signed *okay* happily. I normally would stay up late working on art, anyway, so being together to share ideas would help.

*All right then, how about you all go put on your PJs.* Before we could set up our nest, we would need to get ready for bed, so if we passed out, we would be prepared. None of us had passed out in recent years, but when we started, it would be a common occurrence.

After putting on our sleep clothes, Kyle and Sarah grabbed blankets and pillows from their room. Kyle had sky-blue and navy-blue quilts covered in faint designs. Sarah, on the other hand, had forest-green and dark-brown comforters. We made a large nest like construction in the center of the room stretching to each end of the small area. Dr. Joe had gotten out an almost floor-level table for me to work on while I was on the floor.

As I pulled out a few pieces to finish and for Kyle and Sarah to look over, the table quickly became covered in my artwork. I held out the one I thought Sarah would like and placed it in front of her—the image of a wolf running through a forest on a hunt. The picture was done in grayscale. The moon was shining down on the hunting wolf, the light diffusing through the leaves of the tree.

Next, I grabbed Kyle's piece of a tree with clouds and grass. It was made of different dyed yarn with a speckled look in different sizes. The main colors were green, white, brown, and blue. All of the colors were of varying shades. In the past, Kyle loved such simple pieces, and to my knowledge, as of a month ago, he still did.

I feel a tap on my shoulder, and Kyle was signing. *Could you please add some embroidery along the edges? I think that it might look nice.*

*Sure, as long as you are okay with buying it.* I was looking at Kyle with the sign. I knew Kyle would remember this from the past, but it didn't hurt to remind.

*I am. Could you do it in blue on the bottom and green on the top in a simple loop stich?* Kyle replied quickly, though his signing was still slower than Sarah's.

*Sure, will do. Sarah, do you have any requests for me to edit your piece?* Looking at Sarah, I waited for her response.

She thought for a bit before replying. *I think it might look good if the lighting was darker.* Sarah had a smile on her face as she signed back to me.

*Sure, I can easily edit the shading if I try. So, would you like me to try that? Though remember, since I am editing this piece, you will need to buy it.*

*That is fine, Mark. I wouldn't be asking if I didn't want to buy that piece.*

*Okay, let's get started.* Turning back to the drawing, I pulled out my pencil set, a blending stub, and some sandpaper.

# CHAPTER 13

## *Heading to Sell Art*

It was the morning of the fair, and I was excited. I had a good night at Dr. Joe's house. Kyle and Sarah decided we should do a sleepover in the living room. I worked on my art for most of the night until I fell asleep.

While I was lost in thought, Dr. Joe got my attention by saying my name and stamping his foot. When I got lost in thought, I would lose track of time and not respond to others unless there was a second noise. Kyle and Sarah had already left to get ready in their rooms, and Dr. Joe wanted to make sure I was ready for today. I went over to my bag of clothing and grabbed a pair of soft socks. Next, I grabbed my pair of stretchy black jeans and a soft cotton shirt in a dark tie-dye with my name printed on the front. Grabbing my necklaces, I headed into the bathroom to get dressed.

When I had finished, I was ready except for my shoes. I put on my pair of high tops in a dark tie-dye. I had black shoelaces to go with the hand-painted shoes I made. People would sometimes commission me to paint their shoes so they could have a design that wasn't available in their shoe size. For me, I liked to wear high tops, so I could put more pressure on my ankle. Another thing I liked was how I could have more space to do a design.

Kyle and Sarah came out of their rooms in similar outfits. Both had on jeans and a T-shirt, though the similarities stopped soon after that. Kyle was wearing a hoodie with a design of a forest under stars. Sarah was wearing a sleeveless zip-up hoodie with a picture of a wolf howling at the moon. Kyle was wearing necklaces like me, while Sarah had on bracelets, though more on her left hand, as that was her nondominant hand. She did this to tell which side was her right and left. Kyle had on hiking boots, and Sarah had on sneakers. For both of them, their styles looked nice and fit them and made them comfortable.

Dr. Joe never forced his kids to wear any clothing they didn't like and mostly let them choose their own clothing and styles. Dr. Joe also bought me a few different pieces of clothing as presents. He mostly got me single-color clothing to make customizing easier for me.

All of us were ready, and Dr. Joe was in the kitchen, making breakfast for us before we drove to the church. Kyle and Sarah would often spend time with me at the booth, helping me sell my art. By this point, I had many people who visited and said hi to me. Many just bought in bulk and wouldn't buy again for a couple of months, but they would still say hi.

The people who were my favorites to see when I did these types of fairs were my old teachers. I did also give them a discount on the items they bought as a thank-you to them for working and helping me. I still talk with many of my older teachers if they are still in the area. Some of the schools actually invited me back to talk to some classes, to give them inspiration and to see different opportunities that can be made.

I had lots of fun talking to younger kids and showing and teaching different skills. It is so much fun to see students get excited over a new idea. Part of the passion comes from the kids finally getting a skill and seeing the delight in their eyes for succeeding. These were part of the reason I agreed to go to different schools and do talks and visits.

# CHAPTER 14

# *Setting Up at the Fair*

Leaving Dr. Joe's house, we drove over to the church. The drive was calm and pleasant and didn't take very long. Soon we arrived at the church, and the car jerked to a stop in a parking spot near the entrance reserved today for people to set up booths and transfer goods.

It was time to set up my station. The church gave me two tables to use, along with a small set of cube bookshelves to have behind my tables to hold more of my artwork. I had twelve cubes to work with and a small table to put them on. I began to set up.

I pulled my different binders and placed them on the tables. I had the tables separated into different sections to make it easier for people to find what they wanted. One table had weaving and fabric pieces. The other one had my drawings and paintings. I separated each table into three sections: scenes, characters, and stories. Most of my art was in the scenes, but I also had a good amount of characters on my drawing table, though there were few story pieces. Most of my story pieces were scenes I had drawn for my graphic novel and didn't like the look of, so I decided to rewrite the scene and sell the drawing.

I started by pulling out the weaving and fabric pieces that I used as padding. I pulled out different stands and small blocks to place my pieces on. At the back of my table, I had my large weaving projects. I pulled out my rolled-up nature scene. This was the piece Dr. Joe had bought for his kids that I would be giving them today. It was a rather large piece, about two feet wide by one foot long. It was an image of wolves sleeping on each other in the middle of a clearing. The tapestry used both weaving and embroidery techniques. I used silver thread to separate the wolves slightly and to show the moonlight coming through. This was a layered piece and took me a few days to weave and then sew.

For this tapestry, I used ideas they gave me, and Dr. Joe paid for part of it in advance and was giving the rest to Kyle to purchase. I actually was planning on giving this tapestry as a birthday present, but Dr. Joe wanted to pay me for the piece due to the amount of time it would take to make. Kyle selected this piece last night, and I added some more embroidery to the piece as a finishing touch.

The piece was a beauty; it was mostly in grayscale with a few flashes of color if you looked for them. I hid some blue water droplets under a weave, so that when the weave moved, the water droplets would show. I turned the piece around and hung it on the bookcases so Kyle could see it and buy it.

After I got out that piece, I started to lay down different pieces. I had a few small weighted bags with trees, deer, butterflies, rain, and flowers. I also put down a few small weaves of different pride flags for people to buy. In addition, I had a few smaller patches I made that could be put on bags or clothing. I had a few bags in multiple colors, though for those who wanted more color, I had tie-dyed ones that were slightly larger than the one-color bags.

I pulled out my sewn pieces of mythical animals that were on pillow covers and made to be on blankets. I had a few cloth pieces made to look like they were stained glass in a few styles; most of them were of animals or creatures. I took thin strips of black cloth and hand stitched the different strips in between the different panels to make the effect. The fabric pieces took a few hours to a few days, because all of them were hand sewn. Finally, I had my nature weaves and stained weaves to show nature. These were the easiest technique but, in some ways, the hardest, as the colors needed to be just right.

After I got that table completed, I started on my drawing table. I pulled out my binders, laid them next to each other, and started to pull out specific sheets. Many of the pieces I drew I would only make a set number of, so they would be unique. I finally reached the bottom half of my bag and pulled out my artwork container. I had a few of these to sell if a person wanted a safe container to hold their artwork. In this one I had placed my larger drawing along with the drawing Sarah selected.

The drawing was the same size as the weaving for Kyle and took a little less time. I had drawn a waterspout heading toward a beach with a large cliff. Strong winds pushed rain around in a circle. There was a nearby lighthouse, where the light reflecting through the rain was making a rainbow. The lighthouse was moving around slowly, so there was a ring of light. It showed the different effect of the light on the rain. This was in grayscale, also with small hints of color for the rainbows in some spots.

After that was hung up, I started to put up my other artwork. One was a large picture of a massive tree surrounded by a forest with birds in the sky. I had four copies of this piece for sale. The other large piece was of a cityscape by the water. Between the gaps of the buildings, the ocean could be seen. The buildings were all of varying heights and from different eras. I had nine of these pieces for sale. With all the pieces I made copies of, I would keep the original so there were a limited number of original copies. For the commission-requested pieces I would give the person buying it a few copies and the original drawing and I would keep. All of my artwork had a signature on it to identify it as one of mine.

It was time for the sale to begin.

# CHAPTER 15

## *Selling Art to Old and New Teacher*

People had already begun to stream in while I was setting up, but now it was time to sell. I moved to sit behind my tables on the computer chair I was given. I rolled around happily. Bending down, I took off my shoes and ran my feet on the floor to feel my socks move.

Looking around, I saw many people going to the baked goods tables and then moving to other tables to buy other items after they ate some food. The hall was buzzing with noise, but it was a pleasant type. No one was talking too loudly, and many kids were walking around in noise-canceling headphones. I had my shooting earplugs sitting around my neck, ready to be put in if it got overwhelming. Some kids came up earlier and looked at my different pieces before running off to look at other tables.

If I remember correctly, the parents of that group were trying to get their kids to be more social. Often, I would be invited to different groups to run social craft groups; we would make crafts that kids would need to work together to complete.

I sat waiting with a smile, looking out over different booths and tables, as I waited for my first customer. I saw Mr. David walking up along with Ms. Brown. They worked together and helped plan activities. They were two of the art department heads for the district. They walked up, and we started to talk.

Mr. David signed, *Mark, would you like to communicate in sign or spoken language?* I replied that I was good to speak. "How are you doing, Mark?" I think he said it with a fond tone, though I couldn't tell. "So, anything you want to show us?"

I nodded and reached over to my binders of different scenes and flipped to a few different pages. "I'm doing good. I made some interesting drawings, if you want to see them. How are you doing today, Mr. David?"

"I am doing well, Mark, happy to see that you are well."

I grabbed a couple of different scenery drawings and handed them over. In the pile was a waterfall done in charcoal. I had done the charcoal on a tie-dye-style blue paper with a pineapple-like texture drawn on. This drawing made me excited; I loved doing interesting textures and mixing the texture of water with pineapple was a challenge.

Another piece was of the clouds in a humanoid shape in a nice red and pink spectrum. A few dashes of light blue to show the sky were scattered around. The glare of the sun through parts of the clouds was tricky but manageable. The drawing was designed to look like person peering over a mountain with arms in a fighting position.

The final piece was a tree surrounded by wolves of all different color mixes. Some were white, brown, black. Some had splotches of green, purple, and red due to running and squishing some berries or due to hunting. The tree was relatively young, just starting to grow, and I had drawn the wolves around the tree to look like they were protecting it.

"These are very nice, Mark. I like how you have been experimenting with different textures. You have grown a lot since I first met you. Would it be okay if I bought the waterfall piece you showed me?" Mr. David had a small smile on his face as he was talking.

"Yes, it would, Mr. David. How is class going?" I was wondering, as I worked with some of the kids in his class during a few of my workshops and classes I taught.

"My class is doing great. Actually, that is one of the things I want to talk to you about today."

"What is it?" I tilted my head like I was taught when asking a question.

Mr. David looked over to Ms. Brown, and she began to speak.

"Mark, Mr. David and I would like to invite you to come to a few of the schools and give a lesson to them about what you do. We want to help show some parents that their children can succeed, using you as an example. Many parents are asking for ways they can help their kids to succeed, and we thought you would be a good person to share your experience, how you got help, and what did and didn't help with you succeeding."

I nodded. "Sure, I can help with that. When would it be?"

"It would be during the weekend and after school. The school will give you a few of our older art supplies like a light table, a woodcarving set, and a leather forming and dyeing set."

"Sure, that works. Just give me the times to come and speak."

"Will do. Now, can we go back to the art? How much is this piece?" Mr. David said, holding up the waterfall with pineapple-like texture.

"I actually didn't price that piece. Though, based on the number I made of it and time to make, I would say around thirty dollars."

"I think you're selling this piece short, but if that's what you think it is worth, I'll pay that price." Mr. David was shaking his head at the thought of this.

I just smiled back and replied, "Remember, I give my teachers a discount."

Mr. David just looked at me and smiled while shaking his head.

I heard a large gasp, and I saw my brother standing off to the side looking at us. Mr. David held out money for my artwork. I took the money and placed it in my money box.

# CHAPTER 16

## *Surprise at The Fair*

I SIGHED AND PULLED out one of my cylinders that contained artwork from when Josh first returned from college. He had been happy then and talked with me and took me out to places. Every summer, I add more to this cylinder and continue to grow it with the memories of the good times I have with my brother.

My brother walked up to me with what I thought was a contemplative look on his face. He looked over what I had and looked more confused. Mr. David and Ms. Brown stepped off to the side, offering me silent support and looking ready to step in if they needed to. The distance was growing shorter, until only my table separated us. This was the closest I had been to my brother without wanting to be in range of him since he revert back to the way he was before he went to college. He continued to look over my table before settling on the money box, which had the money Mr. David paid me.

I stayed apprehensive about what would happen. This was the first time my brother had come to one of my art sales. Life had taken a turn, hopefully for the better. My parents supposedly knew of my art sales, but I'm not sure if they remembered. My brother finished looking around before settling on me. He tried to look at my eyes, but I just looked around him. Finally, he settled for looking at my head and began to speak.

"Hello, Mark." He paused. Not knowing what to say before going on. "What are you doing?" His voice was quiet, like he was afraid of the answer, from what I was taught in therapy. Josh, for the first time, was actually acknowledging my work outside of the first few days of summer break.

"I am selling my artwork to the community." I smiled at him. Looking around, I saw a few people focusing on us. Most of the adults around here knew my relationship to my family, so seeing my brother here was an event that most thought would never happen.

"Okay. Are you the one controlling the stand? I heard you tell David how much the artwork was." Josh was looking around scared like this was all a dream. Not knowing what to do, I just continued to answer his questions.

"Yes, I am the one in charge of the stand."

Josh got a strange look on his face and a slightly distant look in his eyes. "Are you making any money from this?" His eyes had begun get hazy, and tears looked like they might start falling.

"Yes, I am. I pay for the space from the church, and I'm able to sell at their fundraiser."

Josh nodded and moved to grab a chair. Around the room the church placed chairs next to the tables for people to sit if they needed to. Sitting down, he rested his head on his hand and just sat. I waited, and finally, after a few minutes, he stood back up and began to speak again, though this time like he was afraid of something happening.

"Mark, I'm sorry. I don't know what to do. I'm glad I came. You are proving everything I knew about you wrong." Josh was smiling now and looking down at my art pieces. I began to pull out different pieces I had drawn to remember the good times with him.

The first one was a small piece on yellow paper of us standing together in front of a store. Josh had taken me to walk around the mall. That day, he bought me a small cord with a small pendant on it. The pendant had three sides, and each side had a different word. The pendant read *strength, love, happiness*. This was in the center of the image in a large bubble with *love* and *happiness* facing outward.

The next piece was on standard white letter paper. It had an image of us at a park next to Kyle's favorite tree, talking. I treasure this moment; it was when I told my brother about a couple of troubles I had, and he gave me advice. The only piece of color in this was the note he gave me on blue paper with advice on what to do. Now that I think about it, I still have that note floating around my room.

I handed Josh these two pieces with a smile. Josh needed to sit down again because of the images. I had forgiven him long ago, but I still have the memories of the bad times. I just like to focus on the good ones. Since leaving for college, Josh hadn't had many bad days unless he listened to a rant from my parents.

Josh placed the two pieces of paper down and moved his hand to his chest and began to sign. *I am still rough at this, but I am learning.*

*Yes, you are rough, but you will get better. Learning is hard, but once learned, it is easy to remember. Why did you start to learn?*

"I didn't get most of that, Mark. I'm sorry."

Mr. David translated that I was asking why he was learning. Josh looked to Mr. David and began to try to speak. Mr. David held up a hand and pointed over to me.

"There is a deaf person that joined my school that I am trying to become friends with. She is very nice and is helping our class in learning how to sign. I only know a few phrases and words, but I am learning."

I smiled at Josh and handed over another drawing. It was in color though muted and the same texture overall. It showed Josh and me standing in front of a craft store and him handing me a crumpled-up twenty-dollar bill. This piece was kind of like a comic, as it was separated into different sections with a few having speech bubbles. The image next to it was of me in the story, looking around for what to get. The next scene was of Josh at the register, paying for something and hiding it inside a bag. The final image was of him giving me a gift that I had been looking at in the store but didn't have the money on me to buy. Josh had a smile on his face and was saying, "Happy first week of summer." That day was the day before I was let out on summer break from school and lost that shelter from my parents and eventually my brother.

"These are all from the first summer I came home after starting college. Why did you make these?" Josh was looking—confused, I think is the word. He had a cautious but hopeful tone. I could recognize this by how telling he was in his voice.

Looking to Mr. David, I asked if he could interpret. Mr. David moved to stand next to Josh, and I began to sign. I felt signing meant more, as that was how I communicate outside of home for the most part, so maybe that would show I was attempting to accept Josh. *I made them to remember the times when you were nice to me. There are a few precious times, though they vanish over the summers as you start to believe our parents again.*

Josh looked slightly ashamed, learning how I felt about him over time.

I handed Josh the large picture from the cylinder. This was a piece of him and me that I drew after last summer. The piece was a collage of us at different places. The main theme was how slowly my smile faded over time as the summer continued. The summer started out with me having a large smile stretching across my face, with us embracing in a hug. Then slowly, over time, the emotion left my face until I was turned into a blank canvas. The physical touches decreased slowly until they were gone, and finally the distance between us grew over time. Each drawing was in front of a different place, each one growing less and less significant to me or my brother, until there was almost no reason to be at that place. Color slowly left the art as the time in the collage progressed, until the last image was in black-and-white.

This was one of the hardest pieces for me to draw; it was two feet long by five feet wide. The drawing and planning of the stages took a few weeks and to put it all together and required a couple of months to make. This was one of my best pieces; it shows my life, and I hope it will help to change Josh's point of view about me. My parents are a lost cause, but I still have hope for Josh being able to become part of my new family slowly as the wounds we had heal.

# CHAPTER 17

## *Sales to Old and New*

JOSH SAT DOWN, GINGERLY holding the large piece. Looking over, I saw his head moving, looking over the paper. Seeing that they were no longer needed, my teachers left, but others stayed nearby. I heard footsteps. Turning around, I saw Dr. Joe looking at Josh. Dr. Joe walked over to him. Something was said, and they began to walk away and ended up in one of the small classrooms nearby, set up as a relaxation room to get away from the noise and colors if needed.

Josh now knew the truth about what I have done since he left. I was nervous to see how he would react once it had all sunk in. Dr. Joe was having a talk with him that has been a long time coming; it would be difficult to hear but necessary. Josh needed to see how I have changed and that I am not the person our parents told him I was.

"Hello, Mark. Do you have any images of can- cani- canni—"

"Do you mean canines, Danny?" Danny was one of the kids I worked with in workshops and after school. I volunteer at the library and teach simple crafts, and his family always attended them. He always made me smile, always happy and asking questions.

"Yes, those ones."

"I do, Danny. What kind are you looking for?" I stepped out from behind my table and knelt, so I was on a similar level to Danny.

"I want a wolf, please."

"Okay, will do. I'll show you my favorite wolf." I pulled down my binder of characters and flipped to one of my favorite drawings. This was a drawing I made for the graphic novel but decided against using. The image was of a large black-and-white wolf with shading to make it look like silver fur was floating around in the wind. Above the wolf, the moon was shining, though the wolf's head was blocking part of it. The moon was low in the sky, and the sun was starting to peek through the trees around the wolf. There were many animals in the tree, looking around, and a small boy standing next to the wolf. This boy was the son of the man looking out at the scene. The man's hand was facing down, pointing at the wolf. On the hand was a ring made of fur stuck in clear resin; it was the same shade as the wolves' fur. This drawing wasn't finished with what I was planning for the book but was finished in terms of me being willing to sell it.

"Could I get this one, Mark?" Danny had a large smile on his face as he looked at the image. I had five copies of this image for sale, and it didn't take me all that long to draw. So, it was twenty dollars.

I would charge him ten dollars if he remembered the coupon, I gave him a few weeks back. Some parents will ask me if I can give their kids a reward for a good job, like a coupon for my artwork, and I normally agree. All I ask is that they donate some art supplies, so I can continue to do the class. Most parents at the start will ask what I need to do to put on the class, as it is all donation based. Then they will bring in what they can for their kids to have fun. Often, I will get many crayons, pens, markers, and colored pencils, along with paper. A few ask about other materials and bring in yarn, paint, canvas, fabric, thread, sewing needles, and more.

"Sure, Danny. Do you have the coupon I gave you?"

He pulled it out proudly and handed it over, waiting for me to tell him how much to pay me.

"All right then, that will be ten dollars for this piece."

Danny's eyes lit up as he handed over the bill and I gave him the piece in a bag along with the paper protector. Danny walked off carefully with his art and a happy smile on his face. I saw Danny's parents looking over at us with a smile, and they gave me a nod and walked away. I could hear Danny happily chatting with his parents about the piece he bought as they explored more of the sale.

I heard a door close, the same door to the room that Josh and Dr. Joe were in.

I felt a tap on my shoulder. I looked over and smiled when I saw a helper from my class. *Hello, Valentine. How are you?*

*I am good, but tired. Any art that is in the style I like, or you recommend?* Valentine was one of the adults who helps me with my art classes.

*Yes, I have a few weighted lap pillows and some texture tapestries that are hard to damage.* They have autism and sensory integration, so they like to have pressure to help them focus.

*Could I get two lap blankets?* Valentine was very helpful in my class, and all the kids liked working with them. Danny viewed us as older siblings and Valentine as an older figure to look up to, because of how much they have had to overcome.

*If I remember correctly, you like solid colors. I have a couple of colors to choose from. So, look it over and let me know what you would like.*

*Could I get the blue and green lap pillows?* Dark colors contrasted with their skin color better, so that did make sense, as it fit with their clothing choice.

I told Valentine how much the lap blankets cost, and they paid for the two of them and moved over. Valentine was one of the people who helped me with my class and gave different info on their demographic identities such as being deaf, nonbinary, and pansexual. They helped my art to be more inclusive. They were part of the reason I made different pride flags, as they helped me sell them to their friends. I would also give them to the different queer-straight student alliances.

I use the info I get when making my art, such as with my commissions, to help me get to know people better. The art is an easy way for me to remember the way people act and interact and types of personalities.

I worked with Valentine often, almost weekly, with my classes, as they are experienced in art and are going to the local community college. They used to help out with the elementary school kids when they were in middle school. They are one of the nicest people I know.

*Could I stay and help you for a bit?*

*Sure, Valentine, whatever you want.*

Valentine moved behind the booth and began to straighten out the pieces I had knocked over while moving my binders.

Two smaller people looking to be around the age of the kids in my class walked up, one looking at the other intently.

*Hello, how are you? My name is Ariel.*

"Hello, how are you doing? My sister's name is Ariel, and I am Jackson."

Valentine and I decided to have a little fun and sign back together.

*Hello, you two. If you would like, we both know sign.*

Their smiles grew. Jackson jumped up and down—I think it was in excitement. Pointing at Jackson, I asked them to come over to me so we could talk.

"Wait, I need to help my sister. She is deaf."

"Don't worry, Valentine will help her. They are also deaf. They know sign, and if they need any help, they will come and ask me."

"But we need to …"

"Don't worry about it. I'm guessing your parents told you to stay near each other?"

"Yes, they did, sir."

"Call me Mark, and look, you two are at the same table. So, what were you looking for?"

"Um, we … were looking for some drawings."

"So, you don't know what you want. How about I show you what I have, and we can continue from there."

"Okay, could I see some of the character drawings? I saw my friend Danny walking around with a cool image of a wolf."

"Sure, I have some different pieces like that. Do you want an animal, humanoid type, or monstrous type drawing?"

"What is humoid?"

"Humanoid, Jackson, though good attempt."

"Humaoid?"

"Close. Try adding the N sound after the A, so it is humanoid."

"Humanoi?"

"Add a D at the end now."

"Humanoid?"

"Yes, that is a being who looks like one of us, like a human."

"That would be great." Jackson had a smile on his face as he looked at me.

I pulled out a few of the pieces from my graphic novel. The pieces were of a few different people. I had the silhouettes of two people looking out into the ocean. One was on crutches, and the other was sitting on the ground with legs spread in front. Off to the side, a group of people was walking up to the group. The moon was just starting to cast its light but was blocked by the cliff, only showing a few streams of moonlight going up.

The next piece was of a person signing. I had a few snapshots of different signs; each of the signs could stand for a few of the different characters. The man was wearing light blue to contrast his dark skin. The piece was in grayscale and had a few dashes of color.

The final piece was of a parent standing in front of a forest with a few kids all standing in a circle. A few of them were signing, and others were walking through the circle or swapping places. This was normal and had a few people in the center signing to help the kids learn the different standards of deaf culture.

"I think your sister might like these two pieces," I said, pointing to the two with people signing. These were sketches I had expanded upon so I could share the language with others or help to show that more people are similar than different.

Jackson pointed to the circle of people signing. Picking up the piece, I gave him a smile and told him it would be ten dollars. Jackson thought for a moment before moving over to his sister. He tapped her shoulder, and she turned around. I was unable to see their signs, as their bodies were blocking each other. After a bit, Valentine came over and tapped my shoulder.

*I think you should do your special deal, since you have never had them in your class before.*

*Good idea. Which of us should tell them about the deal?*

*How about you just give them one of the flyers.*

*Will do. Thank you for the advice, Valentine.*

Valentine nodded and moved over.

I moved in front of the table, tapping them both on the shoulder. I handed over the flyer, signing for them to read it. The paper basically offered a 50 percent discount on the purchase of two items for people still school age if they come to my class within the year or send me a letter saying how they are doing and what they did with the artwork and if the artwork helped them at any hard time.

Jackson and Ariel nodded. Each of them handed over a five-dollar bill, and we gave them the pieces they had been looking at. They left with their purchases, heading over to two parents who had worried looks on their faces at seeing the two pieces. They then handed over the flyer, and the parents smiled and nodded at me.

# CHAPTER 18

# *What is Happening*

THE SALE HAD ENDED. We were there for around three hours. Dr. Joe and Josh had been in the room together for about two hours with the door opening occasionally to look out before closing again. One of the workers put up a do not disturb sign with directions to a different room.

I didn't hear much from that room except for a few loud slams. Valentine or another person would check before coming and letting me know everything was okay.

The door opened, and Dr. Joe walked out and came over to me. He had a smile on his face, though it looked slightly tight.

"Mark, Josh, would like to speak with you about something."

"Dr. Joe, do you think it is a smart idea to go and talk with him?"

"Yes, I do. I'll watch the stand. Just be careful, and remember, we are here for you."

I nodded and walked over to the room, closing the door behind me. Josh was sitting, back straight and head up, looking at me with a focus he had never given me before.

"Hello, Mark." Josh was looking at me, but I refused to meet his eyes. "I'm sorry for how I've treated you. I will attempt to do better."

"Did you practice that with Dr. Joe?"

"Yes, for a little bit, but that isn't what I want to say to you."

"What is it, then?" I asked.

"I'm coming back to this city. Living in an apartment, and I would like you to come to live with me. I want you to leave our parents. I learned what's happened since I left. I am sorry. Please consider this. I called our parents, and they aren't opposed, as long as I continue to, as they said, prevent you from spiraling any more since you stopped listening to them. Please accept and come live with me. I will let you live your life, and you won't have to deal with our parents."

"I will try. Let me pack up, and we can leave."

# GLOSSARY

Accommodations: differing ways to help people to succeed and be on a fair playing level as people without a mental or physical disability.

ADHD: attention deficit hyperactivity disorder.

Advocate: a person who offers help and tries to get people needed help or accommodations. This includes trying to get varying rights for people depending on race, sexual orientation, physical and mental ability, age, gender, and so forth.

Autism: a condition where people have trouble communicating and understanding others' feelings. This makes it harder for them to communicate wants to others or different needs. This can also involve repetitive behavior or actions to try and get sensory information.

Chewies: items designed to be safe to chew on for sensory needs.

Dyslexia: a disorder that makes it harder to read different languages due to mixing up letters or order of words.

Diagnosis: when a person is given information about what they have after testing and observation. This can help led to getting accommodation.

Fidgets: toys designed to be used for stimulation and to help with stimming. Examples are fidget spinners and cubes. They give input to the body in a controlled manner.

Individualized education plan (IEP): A plan designed for the specific student to meet their needs and offer the help needed. Has set specific goals and is a legal document.

Learning styles: different ways of learning. Such as some need movement to learn, hearing the instructions, and seeing the instructions. There are many more, but those are the main types.

Nonverbal: unable to communicate in a verbal manner due to either a mental or physical reason.

Occupational therapy: therapy designed to help with fine motor movements like writing and other skills used in day to day life. Mostly focuses on repetitive motion to help build up strength and muscle memory.

Sensory overload: a response to a situation and either is over simulating or expected to be over-stimulating could have fear or anger involved or a complete shut down of the mind to blank out and restart. The first part with anger or fear is also known as a meltdown. The part about shutting down the mind is also known as a shutdown.

Stimming: behavior to provide stimulus to the body and mind. May form in repeated phrases and actions such as moving hands in a certain way.

Speech therapy: a place where students are taught how to speak correctly and different means of communication if they are unable to speak. One method of non-verbal communication is a communication binder or using sign language.

504s: unlike the IEP, this plan has no specific goals and only gives accommodations. Mostly used for people who broke a limb or don't need the same level of help as a person with an IEP.

www.ingramcontent.com/pod-product-compliance
Lightning Source LLC
Chambersburg PA
CBHW021450070526
44577CB00002B/334